BACKYARD BIRDS OF
California

BACKYARD BIRDS OF California

Bill Fenimore

Gibbs Smith, Publisher
TO ENRICH AND INSPIRE HUMANKIND
Salt Lake City | Charleston | Santa Fe | Santa Barbara

This book is dedicated to my brothers, Len and Larry. They have experienced the natural world with me as we hiked the trails of our youth into our golden years, watching and enjoying the birds.

First Edition
12 11 10   6 5 4 3

Text © 2008 Bill Fenimore
Maps © Cornell Lab of Ornithology
Photo Credits: Gary Aspenall: pages 24, 32, 38, 42, 50; Randy Chatelain: pages 2, 52, 60; Brian L. Currie: page 40; Lee Duer: page 64; Keith Evans: pages 34, 46 (inset), 56; George Jett: pages 22 (inset), 44 (inset); Jerry Liguori: pages 48, 62, 66; Robert R. Ruszala: page 34 (inset); Kelly Thurgood: pages 20, 28, 38 (inset), 46, 54, 58; VIREO: cover, pages 18, 26; Gary Woods: pages 22, 30, 36, 44

Published by
Gibbs Smith
P.O. Box 667
Layton, Utah 84041

Orders: 1.800.835.4993
www.gibbs-smith.com

Designed by Rudy Ramos
Printed and bound in Hong Kong
Gibbs Smith books are printed on paper produced from sustainable PEFC-certified forest/controlled wood source.
Learn more at: www.pefc.org

Library of Congress Cataloging-in-Publication Data
Fenimore, Bill.
  Backyard birds of California / Bill Fenimore. — 1st ed.
     p. cm.
  ISBN-13: 978-1-4236-0348-1
  ISBN-10: 1-4236-0348-6
  1. Birds—California—Identification. 2. Birds—California—Pictorial works.
I. Title.

QL684.C2F46 2008
598.072'34794—dc22
                          2007032203

Contents

Foreword

When I first met Bill Fenimore in 2001, I knew a lifelong friendship was underway. We were about the same age, had grandchildren, and traveled many of the same paths around the world—but that's not what I mean exactly. What struck me most deeply was Bill's infectious enthusiasm for wild birds and his keen desire to share that excitement with others. In many ways, this guide is an inevitable extension of Bill's personality; a natural outlet for his deep appreciation for the satisfactions that come with learning more about wild birds. In this book, Bill has identified those wild birds you will likely see in your own backyard because he knows that your life will never be the same.

In my own work, I often say that the closer we live to each other, the greater we need to live closer to nature. These days, many of us feel the daily pressures of urban or suburban living and yearn for a simpler time when we lived more in tune with natural rhythms and seasonal cycles. We may also feel a tug of desire to live within a smaller framework where we can make a positive contribution to the natural world around us.

In that sense, this guide makes an enormous contribution by revealing new ways to bring more peace and tranquility into our lives by watching and feeding wild birds around our homes.

GEORGE H. PETRIDES SR.
Founder and Chairman
Wild Bird Centers of America, Inc.

Introduction

This guide will enable you to identify and properly name the top twenty-five backyard birds using your backyard bird sanctuary. You will also learn which bird species visit as spring and fall migrants, which are nesting birds, which are winter residents, and which are permanent year-round residents. This guide will educate you about the cover (vegetation), food, and water needs for these birds. It will also show you a variety of ways that you can improve your backyard habitat for birds and the enjoyment you can have watching and caring for them.

Hook Birds

Most birders who develop the enthusiasm that I have can tell you which bird it was that got them hooked. These "hook birds" have been responsible for providing me and others with many years of enjoyment. Some, like me, get hooked early in life. Others don't feel the hook until much later. I have included here two hook bird stories: mine, which happened when I was a young lad, and that of my brother, who got hooked after retiring from a successful career in the United States Air Force.

Bill's Story

When I was ten years old, I saw a strange-looking bird along the Chester River where I was fishing in southeastern Pennsylvania. I had no idea what it was. At that age, I could have told you what a house sparrow, starling, pigeon, or a robin was, but that was about it. This bird was like none of those familiar birds. It was perched on a log overlooking the river, close to the water surface. Its bill was long and pointed. The bird was motionless, like a statue, poised over the water on its perch. It was watching small minnows swimming ever closer to its position. I noticed it was a slender bird, with blue and green feathers on its back. It had a dark cap with shaggy feathers on the back of its neck. The head and neck were a chestnut color.

Suddenly the bird struck. Its bill pierced the water and it came up with a minnow, neatly held at the tip of its bill. The bird quickly swallowed its catch and with a bold abrasive *kyowk* flew off, soon out of sight, around a bend in the river. I stood there watching in amazement as the bird disappeared. *What was that?* I asked myself.

Later that day I was telling a neighbor who was a local schoolteacher about the strange bird. He went into his house and brought out a book about birds. He instructed me to look through the book and see if I could identify the bird that I had seen along the river. Turning the pages of his field guide, I was impressed with the many beautiful birds that were illustrated on each page. Most of the birds were new to me. They had names that I had never heard of before. crossbill, sapsucker, oriole, and so forth. Suddenly, turning the next page, I saw the exact bird I had seen catch the minnow. Excitedly, I pointed it out. "There it is, look," I said. "Why, that's a green heron," the teacher told me. I borrowed the book and studied the green heron's picture the rest of that day. What an amazing bird, I thought. And what an amazing book with all manner of strange birds illustrated in it. That night at the dinner table, I announced to my family that I had seen a green heron while fishing down at the river that day. "What's a green heron?" my father asked me. I pulled out my book and showed him the bird's picture. He stared at it and said, "I've seen this bird before. We always called them mud hens. I never knew their proper name."

I was dumbstruck! As a young fellow, I thought that Dad knew everything. To think that there was something that he didn't know, and that I knew, was a very amazing circumstance. The following day I showed my friends the bird's picture. None of them knew what it was. Well, now I was on to something. I could study this book and learn about birds. Then I could tell my family and friends about them. This was the beginning of my birding hobby, which I have carried on for some fifty-odd years. It has been a very rewarding pastime. It has helped me better identify with nature and appreciate the outdoors.

Brother Len's Story

When I was a kid growing up in Pennsylvania, I only had a mild interest in birds, and that was probably due to my brother's "serious" interest. In those days I remember my brother, Bill, as being the "go-to guy" if you had a question about birds. But my passive interest changed in 1996. Shortly after I retired from the Air Force I joined Bill on a weeklong field trip to Yellowstone National Park. Bill told me in advance to bring along binoculars so that I could better enjoy the wildlife. I expected to see a lot of wildlife. What I didn't expect was to come home with a passion for birding.

On the five-hour drive from Utah to Yellowstone, I noticed that Bill spent more time looking up in the sky than he did looking at the road. "Red-tailed hawk," he would say, spotting a bird soaring high in the sky. Sometimes he would point to a hawk sitting on a telephone pole as we were driving by and say, "Swainson's hawk." His knowledge and skill at being able to identify birds without binoculars (while going sixty miles an hour) impressed me. It wasn't long before he had me doing it. Looking up in the clouds at a bird, I would say, "Red-tailed hawk." Looking at the same bird, Bill would correct me and say, "uh, turkey vulture." *Hmmm,* I would say to myself. *This isn't as easy as it looks.*

We stayed in cabins in Yellowstone's Lamar Valley. Bill quickly befriended another birder. Together they would stop and look at every passing bird and identify it. The excitement and enthusiasm they shared was contagious and I got caught up in the excitement. I would quickly point at a bird flying by that Bill seemed to be ignoring and ask, "What's that?" "Brewer's blackbird," Bill would nonchalantly reply.

After dinner each night we would go out on the porch to watch the wildlife. Under the eaves of the cabin a barn swallow had built a nest. In it were four nestlings. Suddenly an adult flew in, fed each of the begging mouths, and then flew off. Moments later another adult appeared. This went on until dark. To me, it was a magical sight. The next day I saw a mountain bluebird, a beautiful male flying over the field next to our cabin. The bird was the color of the clear blue sky above. I was mesmerized, watching the beauty of the bird as it crisscrossed the field catching insects. At that moment I knew that birding was something I could enjoy.

Since my Yellowstone adventure, my interest in birds has continued to grow. I have traveled extensively across North America and to other countries, learning about birds. I have become an officer in my Audubon chapter, and I even took a Cornell University course on bird biology.

It seems I have found the perfect hobby for my retirement: birding. Thanks, Bill.

Why Feed Backyard Birds?

When I was a toddler, I would watch my mother throw breadcrumbs onto the snow of our Pennsylvania yard for the birds. She felt that the birds needed her help weathering cold winter days. It is still a fond memory of mine, some fifty years later. I became fascinated with those birds as I watched them enjoy Mom's treat.

Birds provide a terrific keyhole into the natural world. Once there, you can wade in as deep as you feel comfortable. Some will be content, like mom, to simply put food out for the birds in winter. Others will want to learn more about the birds, especially identifying them correctly. Still more will desire to learn how they can help birds, as they enjoy watching them. There are others who enjoy birding so much that they continue the knowledge quest by enrolling in citizen science programs, available through the Audubon Society and the Cornell Lab of Ornithology. Whichever category you fall into, birds are wonderful creatures to enjoy.

What Is Backyard Bird Habitat?

When I was a college student, I read a statement in an American history book that I have never forgotten. It created a powerful and lasting image in my mind. The statement was this: "The forest in northeastern America was so dense when the pilgrims landed at Plymouth Rock that a squirrel could travel from the East Coast to the beginning of the Great Plains without ever touching the ground." Imagine that wonderful expanse of natural habitat for the birds that dwelled there.

Today that expansive and contiguous forest does not exist; such has been the impact of development and spread of our rural, urban, and suburban communities. However, it occurred to me as I began to study birds and their habitat needs that there are many "contiguous backyards" throughout America today. Imagine the positive impact we may have on birds by creating a bird-friendly backyard habitat.

What is habitat? Simply put, habitat is cover, food, and water within a reasonable distance from one another. As birds go about their daily activities, the presence of these three elements is essential. Cover refers to the vegetation that exists in a given area. It provides nesting, roosting, loafing, perching, and shelter areas as well as natural foods. Birds will eat nectar, seed, nuts, acorns, berries, and fruits produced by native and cultivated plantings.

Bird Identification

One of the first things you want to do when determining the identity of a bird is to remember the key physical features of the bird that you observed. You can then consult your backyard bird guide to identify the specific bird you have seen, using those physical features noted as clues. Writing down key physical features always helps me remember them more accurately when later reviewing my guide. The advent of digital cameras makes it easier to take a photograph for later study. Making a simple sketch is also helpful. You can make marks and notes on your sketch that will later help whittle down the possible suspect list.

Think of yourself as a detective solving a crime. The witness is being asked key questions to help identify the prime suspect. "Was the suspect tall?" you, the detective, ask. "No," the witness answers, "he was short, about five feet." "What was he wearing?" The witness describes his straw hat, red shirt, and brown slacks. "Did he have any scars or tattoos?" And so it goes, until there are sufficient key clues for you, the birding detective, to positively identify the suspect bird that you observed.

These questioning techniques will be helpful as you use your backyard bird guide. A helpful first step in bird identification is to note the relative size of the bird you observe. Compare it to the profiled bird scale on the bottom of the page. Move forward or backward in the guide until you are in the correct size range of the bird that you have observed. Profiled birds are the hummingbird ($3\,^3/_4$ inches), wren ($4\,^3/_4$ inches), sparrow (6 inches), starling ($8\,^1/_2$ inches), robin (10 inches), dove (12 inches),

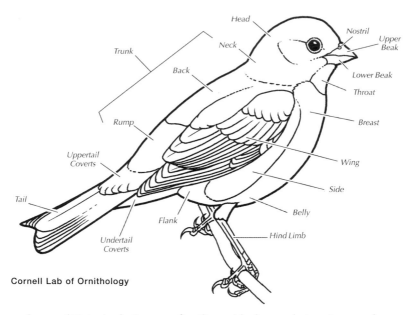

Head
Nostril
Upper Beak
Neck
Trunk
Back
Lower Beak
Throat
Breast
Rump
Uppertail Coverts
Wing
Side
Tail
Flank
Belly
Undertail Coverts
Hind Limb

Cornell Lab of Ornithology

and crow (18 inches). Become familiar with these relative sizes so that you know whether to move forward or backward in the guide.

After noting the relative size of your suspect bird, ask yourself other helpful identification questions. What is the hue of the bird's feathers? Are there any significant identification marks, like the black-and-white-striped crown of a white-crowned sparrow? What is the shape of the bird's mandible (bill or beak)? Is it conical shaped, like that of a house finch? A conical-shaped bill is used for crushing seed and denotes a seed-eating bird. These subtle hints displayed by the bird's physical features will help you narrow the list of suspect birds.

What was the bird doing? Behaviors such as fly catching, drilling into a tree, or eating fruit or nectar are all helpful clues that can separate one bird from another. For example, a robin-sized bird eating fruit could be one of the jays, a bluebird, a mockingbird, a waxwing, or a robin. Taking note that this particular bird's feathers were mostly blue eliminates the mockingbird, waxwing, and robin but leaves the jays and bluebirds. The suspect list is getting smaller.

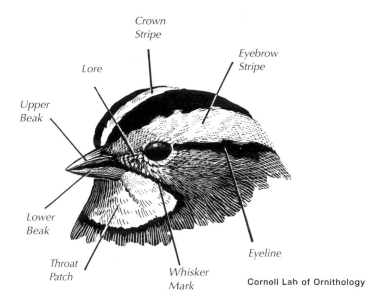

Crown
Stripe

Eyebrow
Stripe

Lore

Upper
Beak

Lower
Beak

Throat
Patch

Whisker
Mark

Eyeline

Cornell Lab of Ornithology

Now check the range distribution map in your bird guide for those remaining suspect birds. The area of the range distribution map where the depicted bird occurs in the nonbreeding season (fall/winter) is colored orange. Summer resident map range distribution areas are colored blue. Green-colored map areas denote permanent year-round residents. This range distribution map will help confirm the presence or absence of the remaining suspect birds: jays and bluebirds. We will use a cold day in February in my native Pennsylvania for our example. The range distribution map for blue jays shows the entire Pennsylvania map colored in green. Aha! Blue jays are permanent residents. The eastern bluebird range distribution range map shows a blue-colored area for the summer. My suspect bird is not likely an eastern bluebird, I begin to think.

Continuing the investigation in our example, I see that the bird at my feeder is eating black oil sunflower seed and it has a crest of feathers raised on its head. Reading the behavior description for the eastern bluebird, I note that it is an insectivore, not a seed eater.

Wing Bars

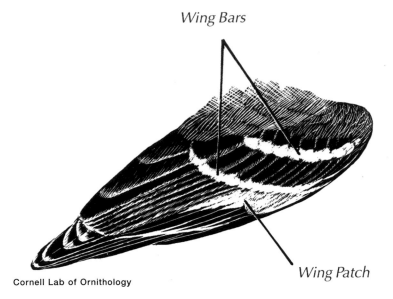

Cornell Lab of Ornithology

Wing Patch

Last but not least, I look at the photographs of both remaining suspect birds, eastern bluebird and blue jay. I can see that the blue jay has a crest of feathers on its head. The eastern bluebird does not show a crest. Now I can confidently see that the bird eating black oil sunflower at my feeder is a blue jay. Its plumage matches the photograph. The crest on my bird is there too. His size is larger than the 7-inch eastern bluebird and the time-of-year range distribution map confirms the blue jay's presence, with the absence of the eastern bluebird in winter.

You will be very pleased to note your progress in being able to sort through the possible suspects until you have determined which visiting bird you are enjoying in your backyard bird sanctuary.

Allen's Hummingbird

Selasphorus sasin

DESCRIPTION: The Allen's hummingbird is only $3^3/_4$ inches long with a wingspan of $4^3/_4$ inches. However, this small hummingbird will attack and defend its territory aggressively. It is fearless and has been known to attack larger birds, including hawks.

You often hear the Allen's wing whistle before seeing it. The adult male Allen's hummingbird is separated from the rufous by its green back. The gorget when flashed is orange-red. The female and immature Allen's hummingbirds are inseparable in the field from the rufous. The Allen's hummingbird migrates earlier in the spring and fall than the rufous.

BEHAVIOR: It is easily attracted to backyard habitats with nectar-producing flowers and nectar feeders. Once it has established a territory, the Allen's will frequent flowers and nectar feeders along an established route. It prefers flowers with tube- or bell-shaped blossoms.

The Allen's will gather insects from spiderwebs and hawk insects on the wing like a flycatcher. Insects are fed to the young as a rich protein source. It will also use sap, as it visits sapsucker wells and collects insects attracted to the sap.

SONG: The Allen's vocalization is a sharp *chip* and twittering *chips*.

HABITAT: The Allen's prefers drier habitats of chaparral, open woods and brushy thickets of parks, and backyard suburbs.

NESTING: Spider silk is used in nest construction with lichen, downy fibers, and other plant fibers. Two white jelly bean-sized eggs are incubated by the female for 15 to 22 days. Young fledge after 22 to 25 days in the nest. Two broods per year.

RANGE: Along the Pacific Coast of California.

SIZE: $3^3/_4$ inches

To Attract: Use a solution of four parts water to one part sugar (4:1) in nectar feeders. Do not add or use red food dye. Boil water two minutes at a rolling boil. Turn off heat. Slowly pour sugar into the hot water while stirring until sugar melts and goes into solution. Cool. Make more than you need and store extra in refrigerator. Change nectar every 3 to 4 days so that it remains fresh. Specialty nature stores offer a convenient liquid nectar or quick-dissolving powder.

Hummingbird	Wren	Sparrow	Starling	Robin	Dove	Crow
$3^3/_4$"	$4^3/_4$"	6"	$8^1/_2$"	10"	12"	18"

Rufous Hummingbird

Selasphorus rufus

DESCRIPTION: The adult male has a rufous back and a dark throat. The gorget flashes a bright red when displayed. Underparts show a white chest with a rufous wash on the flanks and a rufous tail. Females have green upperparts and a white throat patch with small red spots. The underparts are white with a rufous tinge to the flanks.

BEHAVIOR: Rufous hummingbirds feed on the nectar from wildflowers, which it helps pollinate. They will also take insects and spiders, particularly when feeding young, as a source of protein. They will rob insects from spiderwebs and hawk insects in flight. They will also take sap from sapsucker wells and insects trapped in the sap. This is an aggressive hummingbird, not afraid to defend its breeding territory from intruding males.

SONG: *Chip* and chattering. It is often heard before being seen, as the male's wings trill in flight.

HABITAT: Fields with wildflowers; suburban landscapes, gardens, and park areas with flowering plants and vines. Breeds on the Arctic tundra.

NESTING: Female builds a small cup nest from soft plant material, thistle down, and lichen, bound together with spider webbing. It is just large enough to contain the jellybean-sized eggs. Two white eggs are incubated for 11 to 14 days by the female. Altricial young (born naked, eyes closed, and helpless) fledge within 20 days.

RANGE: Spring migration from Mexico north up the Pacific Coast to southern Alaska; inland through the Intermountain West on southern fall migration back to Mexico.

SIZE: $3^3/_4$ inches with a wingspan of $4^3/_4$ inches.

 To Attract: Offer nectar made from water and sugar (4:1 ratio of water to sugar). Do not use red food dye. Boil water 2 minutes at a rolling boil. Turn off heat. Slowly pour sugar into the hot water while stirring until sugar melts and goes into solution. Cool. Make more than you need and store extra in refrigerator. Change nectar every 3 to 4 days so that it remains fresh. Specialty nature stores offer a convenient liquid nectar or quick-dissolving powder. Plant flowers and vines with tube- or bell-shaped blossoms.

Hummingbird	Wren	Sparrow	Starling	Robin	Dove	Crow
$3^3/_4$''	$4^3/_4$''	6''	$8^1/_2$''	10''	12''	18''

Anna's Hummingbird

Calypte anna

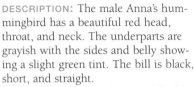

■ Year-round
■ Nonbreeding

DESCRIPTION: The male Anna's hummingbird has a beautiful red head, throat, and neck. The underparts are grayish with the sides and belly showing a slight green tint. The bill is black, short, and straight.

The female Anna's shows red flecks on a throat patch. The crown, nape of the neck, and upperparts are green. The belly and underparts are gray. It has a short black bill. The rounded green tail shows white tips on its outer three feathers.

BEHAVIOR: The Anna's frequents backyard habitats and is expanding its range as backyards and parks are planted with nectar-producing flowers, shrubs, and trees. It readily uses nectar feeders. The Anna's is the only hummingbird seen throughout winter along the coast of California. It prefers flowers with tube- or bell-shaped blossoms.

The Anna's will gather insects from spiderwebs and hawk insects on the wing like a flycatcher. Insects are fed to the young as a rich protein source. It will also use sap, as it visits sapsucker wells and collects insects attracted to the sap.

SONG: The Anna's vocalization is a sharp, squeaky *chick* call. It also will vocalize a rapid rattle during territorial disputes and chases. The male will often vocalize a series of squeaky notes from a dominant perch overlooking its territory.

HABITAT: The Anna's prefers drier habitats of chaparral, open woods, and brushy thickets of parks and backyard suburbs.

NESTING: Spider silk is used in nest construction with lichen, downy fibers, and other plant fibers. Two white jelly bean-sized eggs are incubated by the female for 14 to 19 days. Altricial (born naked, eyes closed, and helpless) when born, young fledge after 18 to 23 days in the nest. Two broods per year.

RANGE: Throughout California, particularly along the coast in winter.

SIZE: $3\,^1/_2$ to 4 inches with a wingspan of $4\,^3/_4$ inches.

To Attract: Use a solution of four parts water to one part sugar (4:1) in nectar feeders. Do not add or use red food dye. Boil water two minutes at a rolling boil. Turn off heat. Slowly pour sugar into the hot water while stirring until sugar melts and goes into solution. Cool. Make more than you need and store extra in refrigerator. Change nectar every 3 to 4 days so that it remains fresh.

Hummingbird	Wren	Sparrow	Starling	Robin	Dove	Crow
$3^3/_4$''	$4^3/_4$''	6''	$8^1/_2$''	10''	12''	18''

Bushtit

Psaltriparus minimus

■ **Year-round**

DESCRIPTION: The bushtit is a tiny plain bird with ash gray upperparts and whitish-gray underparts. Females are separated from males by pale-colored eyes. Males and juveniles have dark brown eyes. The bill is short and black. The tail is long for the body. Coastal birds have a brown crown.

BEHAVIOR: Usually found in flocks that are gregarious, making a light tick and lisping call continuously while moving. Forages by gleaning insects, insect eggs, and spiders from foliage and branches.

SONG: Thin, buzzy twittering and a trilled *sir-r-r-rrrrrr*.

HABITAT: Found in oak woods, pinyon, juniper, and chaparral; suburbs and urban landscapes and parks.

NESTING: Builds a pendulous, gourd-shaped hanging pouch using plant parts, flowers, moss, grass, lichen, hair, feathers, spiderwebs, and insect cocoons. Uses spider silk to hold nest together and to affix nest to an oak branch or shrub. Five to seven white eggs are incubated by both parents for 12 days. Young are altricial (born naked, eyes closed, and helpless) and fledge within two weeks.

RANGE: West Coast and inland into Intermountain West in suitable habitat, down to Texas and into Mexico.

SIZE: $4 \frac{1}{2}$ inches with a wingspan of 7 inches.

 **To Attract:** Plant shrubs and trees that produce berries or small fruits, especially pinyon or juniper, which will also provide foraging and nesting habitat. Reduce or eliminate the use of insecticides.

Hummingbird	Wren	Sparrow	Starling	Robin	Dove	Crow
$3^3/_4$''	$4^3/_4$''	6''	$8^1/_2$''	10''	12''	18''

Lesser Goldfinch

Carduelis psaltria

■ **Breeding**
■ **Year-round**
■ **Wintering**

DESCRIPTION: Smaller than the American goldfinch, the lesser goldfinch exhibits a black cap. Its back is green in the western region and black in the eastern region. It features a white wing bar and displays a white wing patch in flight. The underparts are yellowish-green. The female has blackish wings with two white wing bars. She lacks the black cap and has greenish upperparts with yellowish-green underparts.

BEHAVIOR: A welcome bird in suburban backyards, as it eats many weed seeds. Often found in pairs during summer and foraging flocks in winter. The lesser goldfinch is a gregarious bird that will use open weedy fields, brushy areas, and shrub edges.

SONG: A compilation of twitters, *swee* notes, and warbles. Call note is a *tee-yee.*

HABITAT: Open habitats such as fields, woodland edges, riparian areas, and suburban backyards.

NESTING: The goldfinch is one of the last birds to nest, timing its nesting with the flowering of the thistle. It uses thistle in its nest making. The female builds the nest in a tree or shrub with plant materials, including down, feathers, and grasses. Three to six light blue eggs are incubated by the female for 12 days. Altricial young (born naked, eyes closed, and helpless) fledge within 15 days.

RANGE: California into Nevada, Utah, and Colorado, and south into Mexico.

SIZE: 4 1/2 inches with a wingspan of 8 inches.

To Attract: Offer thistle (Nyjer) and black oil sunflower seed in MoBi Mesh tube feeders or socks available at specialty nature stores.

Hummingbird 3³/₄''   Wren 4³/₄''   Sparrow 6''   Starling 8¹/₂''   Robin 10''   Dove 12''   Crow 18''

American Goldfinch

Carduelis tristis

DESCRIPTION: The American goldfinch is the beautiful yellow "canary" of backyard habitats. Adult male breeding plumage is a bright yellow, set off by black wings with white wing bars and a black cap. The female is a grayish brown with an all-yellow head.

Many backyard observers do not recognize the winter goldfinch when it loses its bright yellow breeding plumage. It molts into a rather drab grayish or brownish plumage so that its energy goes into maintaining the body rather than bright feathers during winter.

BEHAVIOR: The goldfinch is a flocking bird in winter that gathers around backyard feeders and habitats. It feeds on seed-producing flowers, like dandelion and weed seeds. A shallow water feature where it can bathe and drink is a welcome mat for the goldfinch.

SONG: The goldfinch is very vocal, especially in flight where its call note is likened to the mnemonic "po-tato-chip" or "per-chick-oree, perchickoree."

HABITAT: Prefers open areas with trees and shrubs. Backyards provide ideal habitats. Easily attracted to feeders and water features.

NESTING: Nest is woven plant material with plant down, especially from the thistle. The goldfinch incorporates spider silk and caterpillar webbing in its nest construction. Four to six bluish-white eggs are incubated by the female for 10 to 12 days. Fledging takes place within 11 to 17 days. One or two broods per year. Both parents feed young.

RANGE: Throughout the continental United States.

SIZE: 5 inches with a wingspan of 8 to 9 inches.

 **To Attract:** Use Nyjer and black oil sunflower seed. Nyjer seed in socks or MoBi Mesh screen feeders are an ideal way to attract these colorful songbirds.

Hummingbird	Wren	Sparrow	Starling	Robin	Dove	Crow
3¾''	4¾''	6''	8½''	10''	12''	18''

Pine Siskin

Carduelis pinus

DESCRIPTION: Upperparts are brown with a streaked back. Underparts are white with streaking. White wing bar with yellow edging is prominent during flight. Bill is small, pointed, and black. The tail shows a notch, and outer feathers are tinged with yellow.

BEHAVIOR: The pine siskin is a gregarious flocking bird that mixes with the American goldfinch in winter. Siskins feed on Nyjer, black oil sunflower, dried flower seeds, thistle, fiddlehead ferns, and insects. They are a loose colonial nester.

SONG: A sharp rising *zsshreeeee* and trill with a twitter on the end. Call note is a *tweet*.

HABITAT: A wandering nomad during winter irruptions in conifers and deciduous forests, parks, fields, and suburban landscapes.

NESTING: Female builds nest made from moss, lichen, and pieces of bark, feathers, and hair in a conifer, away from the trunk. Three to five light greenish-blue eggs are incubated for 13 days by the female. Altricial young (born naked, eyes closed, and helpless) fledge within 15 days. Both parents feed young.

RANGE: Throughout North American continent in proper habitat in irruption years.

SIZE: 5 inches with a wingspan of 8 1/2 to 9 inches.

 **To Attract:** Offer Nyjer and black oil sunflower in a MoBi mesh feeder available at specialty nature stores.

Hummingbird	Wren	Sparrow	Starling	Robin	Dove	Crow
3 3/4''	4 3/4''	6''	8 1/2''	10''	12''	18''

Oak Titmouse

Baeolophus inornatus

■ **Oak Titmouse**
□ **Juniper Titmouse**

DESCRIPTION: The upperparts of the oak titmouse are gray-brown. The head has a short crest that can be raised. The bill is small and black. Underparts are a lighter gray and the feet and legs are gray-black.

BEHAVIOR: Titmice pair together during the breeding season, and afterward they stay together in small groups and mixed foraging flocks. The titmouse is perky, sociable, and tame. It will occasionally hawk insects in flight, and also consumes seeds and acorns. The titmouse will take a single black oil sunflower to a favorite branch, place it between its feet, and pound it open with its bill like a jackhammer.

SONG: A rapidly whistled high-and-low-alternating *peta-peta-peta-peta.* Call note is a *tschick-a-dee.*

HABITAT: Dry oak woods.

NESTING: The oak titmouse is a cavity nester. Both parents will bring grass, moss, and feathers into a cavity. Six to eight white eggs with occasional reddish brown spots are incubated for 14 to 16 days by the female. Altricial young (born naked, eyes closed, and helpless) fledge within 21 days.

RANGE: Distributed throughout California in oak woods and suburbs that contain good stands of oak trees.

SIZE: 5 3/4 inches with a wingspan of 7 1/2 inches.

✔ **To Attract:** Provide a convertible nest box with a predator guard that will be used for roosting in the winter and nest cavity during breeding season. Offer a nonmelting suet throughout the year.

Hummingbird	Wren	Sparrow	Starling	Robin	Dove	Crow
3 3/4''	4 3/4''	6''	8 1/2''	10''	12''	18''

House Finch

Carpodacus mexicanus

DESCRIPTION: The male house finch has a red forehead. The red wraps around the side of its head over the eyes. The throat and chest are red. The top of the head is brown. The upperparts have brown streaks and the wings display two narrow white wing bars. The chest and underparts have brown streaks. Occasionally the red on males is tinged with orange or yellow. Females and juveniles are a dull brown overall with streaking on the breast and sides.

BEHAVIOR: A gregarious flocking bird in winter. The house finch is one of the more widely distributed backyard birds. It was originally from the West and accidentally introduced to the East in New York in the early 1940s. During winter it will form mixed flocks, particularly with the American goldfinch and pine siskin.

SONG: A three-note rising warble ending with a very high, sharp note. Call notes are *chirps*.

HABITAT: Urban and suburban backyards; parks, gardens, and open woodlands; desert and wooded canyons.

NESTING: Female builds a nest in trees, shrubs, dense bushes, nest boxes, vines, and under building eaves. Uses grass, twigs, feathers, and other material. Two to six light blue eggs with black and purplish spots are incubated by the female for 12 to 14 days. Altricial young (born naked, eyes closed, and helpless) fledge within 19 days.

RANGE: Throughout the continental United States.

SIZE: 6 inches with a wingspan of $9^3/_4$ inches.

 **To Attract:** Offer black oil sunflower in MoBi Mesh tube feeders or hopper feeders available in specialty nature stores.

Hummingbird	Wren	Sparrow	Starling	Robin	Dove	Crow
$3^3/_4''$	$4^3/_4''$	6''	$8^1/_2''$	10''	12''	18''

Dark-eyed Junco

Junco hyemalis

■ Breeding
■ Breeding and winter
■ Winter

DESCRIPTION: There are six forms of the dark-eyed junco. Juncos love to hang out in backyards in winter. They display white feathers on the outer tail when flying.

The "slate-colored" junco is found in the eastern United States. The male has a solid gray head, back, and sides, while females and juveniles are browner. The bill is pink.

The "Oregon" junco is found in the western United States. The male has a black hood, chestnut back, and rusty sides. The female has a gray hood. The bill is pink.

BEHAVIOR: Juncos are primarily ground feeders. Juncos will mix with other songbirds in winter in small foraging flocks. They visit backyard feeders. Juncos eat seeds, insects, caterpillars, berries, and some small fruits.

SONG: A one-pitch trill mixed with *tic* call notes and a metallic, bell-tinkling call.

HABITAT: Conifer and deciduous forests; forest edges; suburban backyards in winter in and around shrubs, hedges, and thickets.

NESTING: A cooperative nest is built by the female from grass, weeds, leaves, and other plant materials gathered by the male. The nest is lined with softer material and feathers. It is usually located on the ground but may be placed in a shrub or tree. Three to six whitish eggs with brown and gray marks are incubated for 11 to 13 days by the female. Altricial young (born naked, eyes closed, and helpless) are fed by the female and fledge within 13 days.

RANGE: Varied forms throughout the continental United States into Canada and northern Mexico.

SIZE: 6 inches with a wingspan of 9 to 10 inches.

To Attract: Offer proso millet, Nyjer, cracked corn, and black oil sunflower seed on a MoBi Mesh platform feeder.

Hummingbird	Wren	Sparrow	Starling	Robin	Dove	Crow
3¾''	4¾''	6''	8½''	10''	12''	18''

House Sparrow

Passer domesticus

■ > 31 birds/route
□ 1–30 birds/route
□ <1 bird/route

No density data

DESCRIPTION: The male house sparrow displays a black bib with a gray crown and cheeks. The upperparts include a chestnut nape bordered with a white stripe and a white wing bar. The back is a buffy brown with black streaks. The underparts are gray. The female has a pale buffy eyebrow line and a plain gray chest with a striped black and brown back.

BEHAVIOR: Hops along the ground as it forages. Gathers in flocks in winter. The sparrow is a loud, gregarious bird. House sparrows eat insects, seeds, grain, and spiders. They will glean insects from tires and grilles of automobiles in parking lots.

SONG: *Chirps* and repeated *cheeps.*

HABITAT: The house sparrow is the bird of the city. It has adapted well to urban landscapes after being introduced in New York City in the 1850s. It quickly spread across the continent and is now found throughout the continental United States, Canada, and Mexico.

NESTING: Both parents build the nest, which is a rough hodgepodge of grasses, weeds, debris, twigs, and feathers. The nest is located in building crevices, nest boxes, vine tangles, and other sheltered areas. Three to seven green or blue eggs with gray and brown spots are incubated by both parents for 10 to 14 days. Altricial young (born naked, eyes closed, and helpless) fledge within 17 days.

RANGE: Across the continental United States and into Canada and Mexico.

SIZE: 6 inches with a wingspan of $9\frac{1}{2}$ to 10 inches.

 **To Attract:** Offer proso millet on platform or hopper feeders.

Hummingbird	Wren	Sparrow	Starling	Robin	Dove	Crow
3¾''	4¾''	6''	8½''	10''	12''	18''

Downy Woodpecker

Picoides pubescens

■ **Year-round**

DESCRIPTION: The downy woodpecker is the smallest woodpecker. Black and white overall, the male has a red nape. The back is white, bordered by black wings, with white spotting on the wings. The face has a black stripe through the eye and a black malar mark. The bill is short, stubby, and half the length of the head (back to front). There are black crosshatch markings on the outer tail feathers (not easily seen). The under-parts are white.

BEHAVIOR: Downy woodpeckers forage in trees for insects and insect egg larvae. They will readily come to suet feeders. When establishing breeding territories, they drum on dead branches and other resonating objects to attract a mate and designate territory boundaries.

SONG: A short *pik* or *chik* call and a soft, high-pitched whinny.

HABITAT: All tree areas, especially suburban backyards.

NESTING: A cavity nester, they will excavate their own cavity and will use a nest box.

RANGE: Found throughout all but the southwestern United States.

SIZE: $6\,1/2$ inches with a wingspan of 11 to 12 inches.

To Attract: Hang suet feeders and a good, formulated, nonmelting suet available at specialty nature stores. Erect a nest box sized for the downy woodpecker with an entrance hole of $1\,1/4$ to $1\,1/2$ inches.

Hummingbird	Wren	Sparrow	Starling	Robin	Dove	Crow
$3\,3/4''$	$4\,3/4''$	$6''$	$8\,1/2''$	$10''$	$12''$	$18''$

Golden-crowned Sparrow

Zonotrichia atricapilla

■ **Breeding**
■ **Wintering**

DESCRIPTION: The golden-crowned sparrow gets its name from the yellow patch on its crown, which is bordered by black head stripes. The upperparts are brownish with brown streaking and two white wing bars. The underparts are a grayish brown.

BEHAVIOR: Found in pairs during the breeding season and in mixed foraging flocks with white-crowned sparrows during winter. It feeds primarily on the ground and in low cover. A variety of seeds, berries, and insects make up its primary diet.

SONG: The mnemonic "oh dear me" in descending notes or "I'm so weary" are the two songs most often heard. Call note is a *chip* and *szeeet*. Sparrows will respond to pishing (a birder's call that arouses their curiosity).

HABITAT: Brushy thickets; woodlands; suburban backyards with shrubs and other low-growing cover.

NESTING: Female builds a ground nest of various plant materials lined with hair, feathers, and soft grasses. Three to five white or whitish-blue eggs are incubated by the female for 11 to 14 days. Altricial young (born naked, eyes closed, and helpless) fledge within 12 days.

RANGE: California north into Canada and Alaska.

SIZE: $7 \frac{1}{4}$ inches with a wingspan of $9 \frac{3}{4}$ inches.

 **To Attract:** Offer proso millet, cracked corn, and sunflower chips on a MoBi Mesh platform feeder, found in specialty nature stores.

Hummingbird	Wren	Sparrow	Starling	Robin	Dove	Crow
3¾''	4¾''	6''	8½''	10''	12''	18''

Black-headed Grosbeak

Pheucticus melanocephalus

■ Breeding
■ Year-round
■ Wintering

DESCRIPTION: Males have a black head with a large conical-shaped bill for crushing seed. The breast and neck collar are cinnamon-orange. The upperparts are black with white wing bars. White wing patches are visible in flight.

The female has a brown head with a white median crown stripe and white stripe (supercilium) over the eye and mustache. Her bill is a heavy conical shape. Two white wing bars. The throat and underparts are a pale cinnamon. There is a lemon wash on the belly.

BEHAVIOR: Black-headed grosbeaks are a Neotropical migrant. They arrive in pairs in the spring and aggressively defend a breeding territory. They inhabit suburban parks and yards, foraging at seed feeders. They will also eat insects, caterpillars, fruits, and berries.

SONG: A melodic robinlike song with a faster cadence.

HABITAT: Found in oak woodlands, backyard habitats with scrub oak and leafy trees, and canyons and riparian habitats.

NESTING: The female builds the nest using twigs, pine needles, and plant material. The nest is lined with soft, fine plant fibers and located in a tree, often near water. Three or four light green-blue eggs hatch in 12 to 14 days. The altricial young (born naked, eyes closed, and helpless) are cared for by both parents and fledge within 11 to 12 days.

RANGE: West Coast and Intermountain West into Arizona and New Mexico.

SIZE: 8 1/2 inches with a wingspan of 12 to 13 inches.

 **To Attract:** Offer black oil sunflower seed in a MoBi Mesh tube or platform feeder.

Hummingbird	Wren	Sparrow	Starling	Robin	Dove	Crow
3³/₄''	4³/₄''	6''	8¹/₂''	10''	12''	18''

Bullock's Oriole

Icterus bullockii

■ Breeding
■ Year-round
■ Wintering

DESCRIPTION: The male Bullock's oriole is a striking bright orange and black bird. It has an orange face with a black eye line and black cap, and black wings with a large white wing patch. The back is black; underparts and rump are orange. Bill is straight and blue-gray.

The female has an olive-brown crown with a yellow face and a thin, dusky eye line. The throat and breast are yellow. Wings are blackish-brown with two white wing bars. The back is an olive-brown and the tail is olive. The underparts are a buffy gray with a weak yellow-orange cast.

BEHAVIOR: Orioles are Neotropical birds. They migrate to the western United States in the spring to breed and raise their young. They migrate south to Mexico and the southern tropics in the fall.

Orioles like to forage in the canopy of trees for a variety of insects and caterpillars. They will also eat berries and fruit. You can attract them with nectar feeders built for orioles.

SONG: A variety of whistles, chatters, and creaks that includes a harsh scolding chatter.

HABITAT: Riparian woodlands; deciduous oak woodlots and woodland edges; gardens and suburban backyard landscapes.

NESTING: Female orioles weave an intricate nest of natural fibers, hair, yarn, string, wool, and grass into a basket shape. Male may help in nest building. They hang the nest from a drooping deciduous branch (often in a cottonwood or willow). Four or five gray-white or light blue oval eggs with black, gray, or brown spots and scrawled black lines are brooded by the female. Altricial young (born naked, eyes closed and helpless) are born after an incubation of 12 to 14 days and fledge from the nest within two weeks.

RANGE: Western Great Plains to the Pacific Coast.

SIZE: 8 1/2 inches with a wingspan of 11 1/4 to 12 1/2 inches.

✔ **To Attract:** Orioles love red hot poker flowers. Hang oriole nectar feeders (4:1 ratio of water to sugar), orange halves, and grape jelly. Specialty nature stores are a good source of oriole nectar and fruit feeders. Place yarn, wool, string, and other natural fiber materials in a suet cage (cut into lengths of 5 to 7 inches). The orioles will pick from these for nesting material.

Hummingbird	Wren	Sparrow	Starling	Robin	Dove	Crow
3 3/4''	4 3/4''	6''	8 1/2''	10''	12''	18''

European Starling

Sturnus vulgaris

■ **Year-round**
■ **Nonbreeding**

DESCRIPTION: The European starling is black overall. The feathers in breeding plumage have a green-purple sheen. The body shape is chunky with a very short tail. The European starling walks rather than hops. Long, thin, pointed bill is yellow in spring and off-white to gray in winter. White spots over body in winter plumage. Juveniles are a dull gray.

BEHAVIOR: This is a flocking bird in winter that can gather in the tens of thousands. The starling is a very gregarious, urbanized bird that has adapted well to the city, town, and countryside. It is non-native to the United States, introduced in New York in 1890. Its diet is extremely varied, including insects, mixed grains, and fruit.

SONG: A variety of whistles, gurgles, clatters, and twitters.

HABITAT: Urban and suburban landscapes.

NESTING: Starlings will nest in natural cavities, nest boxes, buildings, and other structural crevices, such as backyard grills, competing with native species. They will evict woodpeckers from cavities that they have constructed. Nest material is a wide variety of plant material, assembled in a random and shabby fashion. Four to eight blue-green eggs are incubated for 12 to 14 days by both parents. Altricial young (born naked, eyes closed, and helpless) fledge within 18 days. Two to three broods per year.

RANGE: Throughout the continental United States and Canada. The starling is likely the most prolific and abundant bird on the continent.

SIZE: 8 1/2 inches with a wingspan of 15 1/2 inches.

✓ **To Attract:** Will come to suet and seed feeders and will use nest boxes.

Hummingbird	Wren	Sparrow	Starling	Robin	Dove	Crow
3³/₄''	4³/₄''	6''	8¹/₂''	10''	12''	18''

California Towhee

Pipilo crissalis

DESCRIPTION: This is a long-tailed, dusty-brown-colored bird. It has a buffy undertail and throat with fine streaks forming a bib. Juveniles resemble adults and they have two cinnamon wing bars with lightly streaked upperparts and underparts.

BEHAVIOR: Towhees forage in gardens, parks, and chaparral habitats. They sulk under cover, scratching leaf litter in a "one step forward, two steps back" foraging technique. They hop rather than walk. Towhees aggressively defend a territory and mate for life. Mated pairs will bow repeatedly with one another, reinforcing pair bonds.

SONG: Sharp, accelerating, metallic *chink* or *tink* notes in series.

HABITAT: Gardens, parks, chaparral; edge-type areas around developments.

NESTING: Nest located in dense cover and made of bark, twigs, weeds, and grasses, and lined with hair. Two to six light greenish-blue eggs with brown and black marks. Female incubates eggs for 11 days. Altricial young (born naked, eyes closed, and helpless) fledge within 8 days. Both parents continue to feed fledged birds for several weeks.

RANGE: California coastal area populations are declining from development while other area populations increase with edge habitat creation around gardens, parks, and backyards.

SIZE: 9 inches with a wingspan of 11 1/2 to 12 1/2 inches.

To Attract: Provide small seed like proso millet in a MoBi mesh platform feeder.

Hummingbird	Wren	Sparrow	Starling	Robin	Dove	Crow
3 3/4''	4 3/4''	6''	8 1/2''	10''	12''	18''

American Robin

Turdus migratorius

DESCRIPTION: Perhaps the most recognized backyard bird in North America, the American robin is widely distributed throughout the continental United States. Although thought of as a harbinger of spring, the robin is found throughout the year in most of its range. It will migrate south of the snow line in winter when snow exceeds four inches in depth.

The robin features a brick-red breast. It has a yellow bill with a broken white eye ring. The throat is white with black striping. The back is gray. Juveniles when first fledging from the nest have a spotted chest and underparts; otherwise they resemble adults.

BEHAVIOR: Spring finds males fighting and defending territories that are made up of various neighborhood yards. Males will often fight their shadows in low windows in spring. They are often seen probing the yard for earthworms and other invertebrates. Robins switch to a fruit and berry diet in winter when worms are not available. Solitary or in pairs in spring, robins gather in large communal flocks in winter.

SONG: A very vocal singer, often into the night with its repeated "cheerily cheer-up cheerio" phrase. Vocalizations vary with a whinny and sharp warning *tut-tut-tut.*

HABITAT: Urban/suburban lawns and yards with trees and shrubs.

NESTING: A classic round grass nest with a mud bottom located in the fork of a tree. Will use a nesting shelf. Robins usually locate their first nest in a conifer (it already has its leaves in early spring). A second nest and brood is raised in a deciduous tree that has leafed out by early summer. Occasionally, a third brood is raised. Three to seven sky blue eggs are incubated by the female for 12 to 14 days. The altricial young (born naked, eyes closed, and helpless) fledge within 14 to 16 days.

RANGE: Throughout the continental United States.

SIZE: 10 inches with a wingspan of 14 to 16 inches.

 **To Attract:** Plant fruit- and berry-producing shrubs and trees that robins can use in spring and winter, such as mulberry, crabapple, pyracantha, and mountain ash. Robins will use suet if it is presented so that they can perch to reach it.

Hummingbird	Wren	Sparrow	Starling	Robin	Dove	Crow
3³/₄"	4³/₄"	6"	8¹/₂"	10"	12"	18"

Northern Mockingbird

Mimus polyglottos

■ **Year-round**

DESCRIPTION: The northern mockingbird is an overall gray bird with two white wing bars that become large white wing patches when seen in flight. The tail is long and has white outer tail feathers.

BEHAVIOR: A fairly common bird in its range that forages in and around shrubs, trees, and edges of gardens and backyards. It eats insects, fruit, and berries. Vigorously defends nesting area, attacking any animal, bird, or person passing nearby. Often seen running on ground and flashing wings to flush insects.

SONG: The mockingbird is a mimic that sings and imitates other sounds and birdsongs. Repetitive phrases sung with a loud *tchack* call. Mockingbirds will often sing all night during breeding season.

HABITAT: Suburban landscapes; parks, gardens, and farms. Well adapted to living among backyard habitats.

NESTING: Both parents build nest in a shrub or tree with a variety of sticks, twigs, leaves, and string, lined with softer plant materials. Two to six bluish-green eggs spotted with brown are incubated by the female for 12 to 13 days. Altricial young (born naked, eyes closed, and helpless) fledge within 13 days.

RANGE: Eastern and southwestern United States into California.

SIZE: 10 inches with a wingspan of 13 to 15 inches.

To Attract: Offer suet and dried fruits. Plant trees, shrubs, and vines that will produce persistent crops of berries and fruit.

Hummingbird	Wren	Sparrow	Starling	Robin	Dove	Crow
3³/₄''	4³/₄''	6''	8¹/₂''	10''	12''	18''

Western Scrub Jay

Aphelocoma californica

DESCRIPTION: Blue head with a white eyebrow. The throat is white with a blue streaked necklace. Back is gray with a brown saddle, and wings and long tail are blue. Underparts are a grayish white. The legs and feet are black.

BEHAVIOR: The western scrub jay is found in pairs in spring and then in small flocks after breeding and the young become independent. Scrub jays forage in woodlots, suburban landscapes, open park areas, and forest edges. They are opportunistic feeders that have a widely varied diet, including insects, seeds, mice, frogs, berries, fruits, eggs, and nestlings of other birds.

SONG: A strong repeated *shroop* and *shek-shek-shek-shek* in harsh tones.

HABITAT: Forests, woodlots, parks, and suburban landscapes.

NESTING: Both parents build nest from twigs, sticks, grass, moss, and softer plant material in a tree or shrub. Two to seven light grayish-green eggs are incubated by the female for 15 to 17 days. Altricial young (born naked, eyes closed, and helpless) fledge within 19 days.

RANGE: Pacific Coast and inland through Intermountain West.

SIZE: 11 inches with a wingspan of 16 inches.

To Attract: Offer black oil sunflower seed in a hopper feeder and shelled peanuts and tree nuts in a MoBi Mesh feeder available at specialty nature stores.

Hummingbird	Wren	Sparrow	Starling	Robin	Dove	Crow
3³/₄"	4³/₄"	6"	8¹/₂"	10"	12"	18"

Mourning Dove

Zenaida macroura

■ Breeding
■ Year-round
■ Nonbreeding

DESCRIPTION: The mourning dove is a brownish-gray bird with black spots on the upper wing. Male doves show a pinkish tinge on the breast and a black spot on the cheek with a blue-gray crown. The tail is long and all of the tail feathers are tipped in white on the ends. The female is a faded brown. Juveniles have a scaled appearance.

BEHAVIOR: Males will aggressively defend breeding territories. Doves will form flocks after breeding season. They feed on a variety of seeds and grains. Wings make a whistling sound during takeoff.

SONG: A mournful *coo* repeated *cooo, cooo, cooo, cooo* by the male in breeding season.

HABITAT: Fields, agricultural areas, parks, gardens, and suburban backyards.

NESTING: The female pulls together a loose assortment of twigs that makes a flimsy platform in a tree or shrub. Two white eggs are incubated by both parents for 14 days. Altricial young (born naked, eyes closed, and helpless) fledge within 14 days. The young squab is fed crop milk, which is produced in the crop and regurgitated with seeds. Several broods are raised during the breeding season.

RANGE: Throughout the continental United States and into Canada and Mexico.

SIZE: 12 inches with a wingspan of 17 to 19 inches.

 To Attract: Offer black oil sunflower seed, cracked corn, or proso millet on a platform feeder.

Hummingbird	Wren	Sparrow	Starling	Robin	Dove	Crow
3¾''	4¾''	6''	8½''	10''	12''	18''

Northern Flicker (Red-shafted)

Colaptes auratus

■ Breeding
■ Year-round
■ Wintering

DESCRIPTION: The northern flicker is a large woodpecker with underwing colorations that differ based on its geographical distribution. The "yellow-shafted" form occurs from northern Canada into the Midwest, down into the Gulf states, and north throughout the East and New England. The "red-shafted" form occurs in the western United States. When it is in flight, the flicker shows the flashing yellow or red underwing. The flicker also has a rounded white rump patch shown in flight on top of its back where the tail joins the body. The bill is a long and stout chisel.

The male red-shafted flicker has a red mustache. The male yellow-shafted flicker has a black mustache and a red crescent on the back of the neck. Both forms have a gray-brown crown, face, and nape. The upperparts are brown with black barring. The underparts show a prominent black bib with scattered large dark spots on a white chest and belly. Females lack the mustache.

BEHAVIOR: Flickers are most often seen on the ground, where they forage for ants. When ants are not available in winter they frequent backyards with suet. Flickers drum in spring to establish breeding territories.

SONG: A loud and bold *wick-er, wick-er* note repeated and a sharp *kleeyah* note for the call.

HABITAT: Widespread throughout forests, parks, gardens, and backyard suburban landscapes.

NESTING: Both parents excavate the cavity that can be in a dead snag, pole, or a nest box. Three to twelve white eggs are incubated by both parents for 11 to 16 days. Altricial young (born naked, eyes closed, and helpless) fledge within 28 days.

RANGE: Across Canada and the continental United States into Mexico, distribution varying by form.

SIZE: 12 3/4 to 14 inches with a wingspan of 19 to 21 inches.

To Attract: Offer suet on a tail prop suet feeder and peanut splits in a MoBi Mesh peanut feeder found at specialty nature stores.

Hummingbird	Wren	Sparrow	Starling	Robin	Dove	Crow
3 3/4''	4 3/4''	6''	8 1/2''	10''	12''	18''

Sharp-shinned Hawk

Accipiter striatus

■ **Breeding**
■ **Breeding and wintering**
■ **Wintering**

DESCRIPTION: The upperparts of the adult sharp-shinned hawk are blue-gray. The underparts show a finely streaked throat with red barring across the chest and belly. Juveniles have brown upperparts with striped underparts. Mature birds have a red eye. The undertail coverts are white. The tail is banded and ends with a small white terminal band. Tail is squared off in flight.

BEHAVIOR: Accipiters are the 100-yard dash, high-hurdle runners of the bird world. The sharpie is like a fighter jet. It is built for short bursts of speed, cutting, wheeling, and making sharp turns in and around shrubs, trees, and other cover. It hunts and catches other birds on the wing. It often uses an ambush strategy, hunting from a perch.

SONG: *Kee-kee, kee-kee,* given as an alarm call.

HABITAT: Dense woods and woodlots; suburban landscapes with trees.

NESTING: A well-constructed and strong nest made up of twigs, sticks, and small branches. The nest is lined with softer material, including grass and pine needles. Four or five white to bluish eggs are incubated by the female for 32 to 35 days. Semialtricial young (born with eyes open or closed, down covered, and nest bound until fledging) leave the nest within 27 days.

RANGE: Throughout North America.

SIZE: 10 to 14 inches with a wingspan of 20 to 28 inches.

Hummingbird	Wren	Sparrow	Starling	Robin	Dove	Crow
3³/₄''	4³/₄''	6''	8¹/₂''	10''	12''	18''

American Crow

Corvus brachyrhynchos

DESCRIPTION: The American crow is a large, entirely black bird from head to toe. It is one of the most widely distributed birds in North America. Crows are very intelligent birds that have adapted and persisted throughout their range. The fan-shaped tail, squared off at the end, is a good field mark in flight, separating it from the larger raven.

Extended family groups frequent a summer range. Crows are most often found in flocks that can be quite large during migration and in winter roosts.

BEHAVIOR: The American crow will eat a wide variety of foods, essentially anything that it can swallow and digest, including bird eggs and nestlings. This varied diet is one reason why it is so successful. Crows will mob hawks and owls.

SONG: The *caw-caw* of the adult is readily recognized. Its repertoire of *caws* and *caw* variations make its vocabulary extremely large.

HABITAT: Once a rural agricultural-based bird, it has found fast food and urban/suburban landscapes to its liking.

NESTING: Nest is made up of branches and twigs, lined with grass, feathers, and tree bark. It is usually located in the fork of a tree. Four or five bluish-green eggs are incubated by both parents for 18 days. Young are altricial (born naked, eyes closed, and helpless) when born. They fledge within 28 to 35 days.

RANGE: Throughout the continental United States.

SIZE: 18 inches with a wingspan of 33 to 40 inches.

 **To Attract:** Crows will use a platform feeder and enjoy suet. Use tube-shaped perching-style feeders to dissuade crows from other birds' food.

Hummingbird	Wren	Sparrow	Starling	Robin	Dove	Crow
3¾"	4¾"	6"	8½"	10"	12"	18"

Cooper's Hawk

Accipiter cooperii

DESCRIPTION: The adult Cooper's hawk exhibits blue-gray upperparts and light reddish bars on the chest and underparts. The undertail covert feathers are white. Juvenile has streaked underparts and brown upperparts. Tail is banded with a white terminal band. In flight, the tail appears rounded at the end and the head projects in front of the leading edge of the wing. Adult birds have a red eye.

BEHAVIOR: Accipiters are the 100-yard dash, high-hurdle runners of the bird world. They are built for short bursts of speed, cutting, wheeling, and making sharp turns in and around shrubs, trees, and other cover. They hunt and catch other birds on the wing. Cooper's hawks will also catch small mammals. They often use an ambush strategy, hunting from a perch.

SONG: Alarm call is a *keh-keh-keh* or a *kac-kac-kac* given near the nest.

HABITAT: Woodlands, parks, and backyards with trees mixed with woody shrubs.

NESTING: Both parents are active in nest building, incubation, and feeding of the young. A large nest is located in the crotch of a tree near the trunk. The nest is made with twigs and larger sticks and lined with wood chips and bark. Four or five bluish or greenish eggs with brown spots are incubated for 32 to 36 days. The semialtricial young (born with eyes open or closed, down covered, and nest bound until fledging) leave the nest within 34 days.

RANGE: Throughout the continental United States and into southern Canada.

SIZE: 14 to 19 inches with a wingspan of 28 to 34 inches.

Hummingbird	Wren	Sparrow	Starling	Robin	Dove	Crow
3¾''	4¾''	6''	8½''	10''	12''	18''

FEEDING PREFERENCES
OF FAVORITE BACKYARD BIRDS

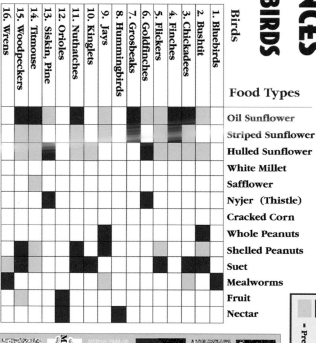

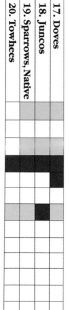

Birds

Perching Birds

1. Bluebirds
2. Bushtit
3. Chickadees
4. Finches
5. Flickers
6. Goldfinches
7. Grosbeaks
8. Hummingbirds
9. Jays
10. Kinglets
11. Nuthatches
12. Orioles
13. Siskin, Pine
14. Titmouse
15. Woodpeckers
16. Wrens

Ground Feeding Birds

17. Doves
18. Juncos
19. Sparrows, Native
20. Towhees

Food Types

- Oil Sunflower
- Striped Sunflower
- Hulled Sunflower
- White Millet
- Safflower
- Nyjer (Thistle)
- Cracked Corn
- Whole Peanuts
- Shelled Peanuts
- Suet
- Mealworms
- Fruit
- Nectar

Legend:
■ = Most Preferred
▨ = Preferred

MEALWORMS · Millet · Safflower · Suet · Nyjer · Striped Sunflower · Black Oil Sunflower

Reference Materials

Supplemental feeding

Some backyard birds are ground-feeding birds. Native sparrows, like the dark-eyed junco, towhee, dove, quail, and pheasant naturally feed on the ground (i.e., a flat surface). Others are considered perching birds, like the colorful American goldfinch, house finch, and black-capped chickadee. These birds like to feed from a perching position.

Understanding a bird's preferred feeding style and behavior guides us toward the proper style of bird feeder selection. A platform feeder is an imitation of the ground that sparrows, doves, and quail will readily use. Scattering the right seeds on it, since these birds are seed eaters, will provide an attraction that they will soon come to enjoy- -seed on a flat surface. A tube feeder with perches will attract perching birds: finches, chickadees, and goldfinches

Positioning feeders at different height levels— hanging from tree limbs, on the ground, and in intermediate height areas—will provide birds with varying space dimensions that mimic natural feeding and foraging behavior. Place feeders where they can be easily watched and enjoyed as you observe the birds attracted to your backyard bird sanctuary. A nectar feeder placed in a flower bed around a patio area can provide delightful entertainment as you watch hummingbirds and orioles visiting the flowers for their nectar, as well as your sugar water.

Remember that there are more species of birds than just seed-eating birds. Provide sugar water in nectar feeders. There are a variety of feeder styles available that will enable you to present a wide assortment of food for the birds visiting your backyard bird sanctuary. There are feeders made to present mealworms, suet, fresh or dried fruit, jelly, tree nuts, and peanuts, in addition to a wide assortment of seeds. This variety of feeders and food assortment will help you attract a wide variety of birds.

What Do I Feed Birds?
Where Do I Put My Feeder?

UP

Suet

Nyjer

Nectar

Mealworms

Oil Sunflower up

Perching Birds

Millet and mixes down

Ground Feeding Birds

DOWN

The Rule: Sunflower up. Millet Down.

The Question: Where do you want to watch birds from?

Warblers, vireos, and bluebirds will come readily to feeders offering mealworms. Woodpeckers and other insect-eating birds will be attracted to suet. Chickadees, finches, and siskins are just a few of the birds that will come to seed feeders. Orioles, robins, and mockingbirds are readily attracted to fruit, berries, and jelly.

Attracting and Understanding Hummingbirds

The hummingbird is a marvel of nature. You will never forget the first time you see one of these flying jewels visiting your backyard bird sanctuary.

Hummingbirds are attracted to and return to feeders that contain nectar resembling flower nectar. This nectar can be made at home with four parts boiling water to one part table sugar. Dissolve sugar in water and allow to cool to room temperature. Store for up to four weeks in a clean sealed jar in your refrigerator. Hummingbirds like fresh nectar, so only place enough nectar in your feeder that will be consumed in three days. Nectar sours in about four days when over 80 degrees F. Do not use red dye, honey, juice, fructose, artificial sweetener, brown sugar, or syrup in hummingbird nectar. These are dangerous to hummingbirds.

Nectar-producing flowers are very attractive to hummingbirds. Some of these that you may plant include: trumpet vine, columbine, honeysuckle vine, red penstemon, cardinal flower, bleeding hearts, bee balm, fuchsia, coral bells, and scarlet sage.

East of the Mississippi River there is only one type of hummingbird, the ruby-throated hummingbird. West of the Mississippi River there are several species, depending on your location and suitable habitat: Allen's, Anna's, black-chinned, broad-tailed, calliope, Costa's, and the rufous hummingbird. The rufous hummingbird is copperlike in color. The male is a big bully at the feeder. The black-chinned male has a dark, almost black head and throat. The broad-tailed male has a green head and garnet throat. The calliope is the smallest hummingbird in North America. The male has a garnet-streaked throat with a green head.

Mealworms for Birds

Mealworms can entice a bird to use a nearby nest box. They help an incubating female find food quickly, so her eggs are not left for long periods of time. Mealworms provide protein for nestlings, and they help birds survive during spells of severe winter weather, when food is hard to find. They are clean, easy to care for, do not carry human diseases, and are readily accepted by birds.

Keep mealworms in a refrigerator. Do not allow them to freeze; take them out every five to seven days. Allow them to warm up and start moving around (takes about one to two hours). Place cubes of apple $1/4$ inch in size in with them and leave for another one to two hours. Refrigerate again. Remove old apple cubes when you take out for next warming-and-feeding period and replace with new apple cubes.

In your backyard, place the mealworm feeder in the open, clearly within a bird's view. Place the feeder near existing feeding areas so that the birds will be able to easily find the new treat. Many birds are attracted to mealworms, including the black-capped chickadee, Bullock's oriole, black-headed grosbeak, robin, cedar waxwing, western scrub jay, downy woodpecker, northern flicker, house wren, house finch, and goldfinch.

Protecting birds from cats and other predators

Place feeders where they are not within an easy leap of an ambush spot. I like to place ground feeders at least two cat bounds away from any cover. This provides the feeding birds an opportunity to detect and escape the cat. Cats are not native to this country. Birds have not evolved with domesticated cats, so they do not readily recognize them as dangerous.

Another method I use to provide added safety for the birds coming to my backyard bird sanctuary is to place a short garden fence with a large wire grid around the bird-feeding area. The large grid opening in the fencing allows the birds to come and go easily. The short fence is easy for me to step over when refilling feeders. However, it is a barrier that the charging cat must navigate. This provides the birds with more opportunity to elude the cat.

Keeping a cat inside the house is the very best way to keep and enjoy a cat. They live longer lives when kept inside, avoiding accidents with vehicles and harassment from other critters, and they can safely enjoy watching birds through the window.

Bird baths and the importance of water

A bird bath is perhaps the easiest way to provide the greatest diversity of bird species visiting the backyard. Many migrating birds will stop to

bathe and drink. Resident birds will soon learn of reliable local water features. They will visit the bath regularly

When birds learn of a reliable open water source in winter, when all other water is frozen solid, they will "flock" to your backyard bird sanctuary. You will be delighted with the diversity and number of birds visiting your water feature. My wife called me recently one cold winter day to show me the twenty-five American robins using our bird bath. There were several more perched nearby, awaiting their turn at the "bird spa." You can keep your bird bath water from freezing with a heating element. If you are planning to purchase a bird bath, look for styles that incorporate a heating element that is controlled with an internal thermostat. If you already own a bird bath, you can buy a heating element that is designed for use in a bird bath. It is a good investment. The birds will be the benefactors. You will be too, just as Mom and I were as we enjoyed watching our visiting birds.

Regular bathing is important for the birds. They must bathe, clean, and preen their feathers to keep them aerodynamically fit. Clean feathers are better insulators that enable the bird to trap air. The air is heated by the body, which keeps the bird warm during those cold winter days and nights.

Water in a bath should have a depth ranging between $1/2$ inch and $1 \, 1/2$ inches. Any deeper is of little use to birds. Birds prefer water at ground level, so the higher off the ground the bath, the less birds will use it. Fresh, clean water is attractive to birds, not dirty, algae-filled water. The more natural the water feature looks, the more birds will use it.

Remember:
> Standing water is good
> Dripping water is better
> Misting water is great
> Moving water is best

Birds are especially vulnerable while bathing. Wet feathers will slow their take-off and flight considerably. Therefore, birds are very cautious while bathing. Provide a safe bathing site for them, and they will use it. A bath out in the open without any cover nearby (two to four feet away) makes a bathing bird vulnerable to attack from a bird of prey.

Pishing

Pishing is an onomatopoeic squeak, squeal, or stuttering slur emitted by a birder to lure a bird hidden from view into the open. Everyone is familiar with the famous saying: "A bird in hand is worth two in the bush." A birder would say "a bird in view in the bush is all I desire."

Often you catch a blur of movement in the yard as a bird flits into the cover of a nearby hedge or shrub. Some birds are natural skulkers, fox sparrows and catbirds for example.

You wait but it will not come into view. The mystery bird is quiet, so there is no song to identify. You are not quite sure what bird it is. Yet you crave a view to satisfy your quest to know and identify it. Hence, you rely on your ability to pish, i.e., coax the bird out of the cover and into view.

Many birds will respond to alarm or mobbing calls out of curiosity. Chickadees, wrens, and nuthatches are particularly piqued by pishing. I use four types of pishing:

A low sounding *pish-pish-pish,* as I force air against my lips with clenched teeth. The air pushes my lips open and utters the pishing sound. Slow and low pishing in groups of three notes is usually sufficient.

My second style is a louder, more rapid series *pish-pish-pish,* with teeth slightly apart and lips closed. The force of air pushes my lips open, as if giving a kiss.

The third manner is to kiss the back of my hand while sucking air into my mouth. The loud squeak is repeated.

Sparrows respond best to a loud and sharp *chip* note. Hold your middle and index fingers against closed lips and give a high-pitched kiss. Repeat this kiss *chip* sound at one-second intervals for four or five notes.

Once you have lured the bird into view for identification, stop pishing. Don't overuse pishing, since you do not want to tax the birds or distract them from their daily routine.

Cover

Cover is the vegetation that exists in your yard that creates suitable habitat for birds to live. A key use of cover is for nesting. Besides feeding and bathing, birds need to have a safe place where they can make a nest and raise their young. Nesting cover can be shrubs, trees, vines, and other similar growth that gives the birds a structure to build a nest where they can safely lay eggs, incubate, and fledge their young. Some birds are ground nesters, such as pheasants and quail. Other birds build a nest off the ground, such as the robin and oriole.

Then there are the cavity nesters. Cavity nesters like the woodpecker can drill and excavate a cavity in a tree. They will make a new cavity each year. Creating a cavity is a part of the bonding ritual that the birds go through. Males show potential mates that they can acquire and defend a breeding territory. They will attract a female to their territory by showing existing cavities. The female visits and decides whether she will nest there. It is usually the female who builds and constructs the actual nest. Other cavity nesters will use old woodpecker holes or natural cavities. Some will excavate their cavities like the woodpecker. You can also erect a nest box to simulate the cavity. Erecting a nest box will give you the opportunity to provide suitable habitat for these interesting birds.

Nest Box Building

Nest boxes serve as a replacement of the natural cavity that cavity-nesting birds seek out. Placing nest boxes in suitable habitat enables cavity nesters to raise their young. The nest box also gives us an opportunity to enjoy the birds during this critical time in their lives.

Which bird will live in a particular nest box is determined primarily by the size of the entrance hole. Beyond that, there are recommended interior dimensions for the various species that make up the cavity-nesting birds. The following list includes some of the birds who are cavity nesters: chickadee; northern flicker; downy and hairy woodpecker; Williamson's and red-naped sapsucker; white-breasted, red-breasted, and pygmy nuthatch; juniper titmouse; western screech owl; house wren; eastern, mountain, and western bluebird; starling; house sparrow; tree swallow; American kestrel; and wood duck.

Remember that a nesting bird wants its nest to be secluded, out of the hustle and bustle of other birds, animals, and people. Don't locate your nest box next to your bird feeder or birdbath. Do not place a perch below the entrance hole. Other birds will use it to harass and worry the birds inside. A mother bird may abandon a nest if she is stressed in such a manner.

A nest box needs to be cleaned out in the fall after each nesting season. More than two broods may be raised within a season, so wait until fall to clean it out. Hang the nest box so that it gets morning sun. Place the entrance hole facing northeast, east, or southeast. The entrance hole should not receive afternoon sun. Place clean wood shavings or chips in chickadee and nuthatch nest boxes. Woodpecker boxes can be filled with shavings or chips so that they can "excavate" the box. This method prevents European starlings from entering a nest box.

Most boxes can be hung at "Grandpa's hoisting height." This is the height that I can lift up my grandkids so that they can see what is happening in the box without my needing to climb up a ladder with them in tow.

One particularly enjoyable nest box to place in your backyard bird sanctuary is the convertible nest box. It is a uniquely designed nest box that can be used by birds year-round. The nest box entrance hole located on the front panel of the nest box can be swiveled back and forth from the top (up) to the bottom (down) of the nest box depending on the season of the year. During spring the nest box entrance hole is placed in the top (up) position. The ventilation holes located high up on the side panels are placed in the open position. A small mesh wire platform is placed inside on the floor of the nest box. Hot air rises. This configuration facilitates free air flow through the nest box. There is a Plexiglas side panel that can be opened to inspect activity inside the nest box. You will delight when you open this panel and see a nest with eggs or young nestlings inside. After the nesting season is over in the fall, you reverse the entrance hole to the bottom (down) position on the front of the nest box. Next you close the vents on the inside panels and remove the old nest. It is important to remove the old nest from the nest box. It makes the nest box ready for new nest construction the following spring. Building a new nest is a part of the bonding ritual of the breeding birds using the nest box.

Now the nest box is snug and ready for winter. There are two peg perches on the inside of the box that are raised up off the floor above the entrance hole that is now at the bottom of the nest box. These will serve as perches for winter roosting birds. Cold air sinks. Roosting birds perched on the two pegs will have their body heat trapped in the upper chamber of the nest box (remember that hot air rises). This arrangement will keep them warm and protected from the cold of long winter nights. The entrance hole has a metal strip around the outside edge so that squirrels or raccoons cannot chew the hole to make it wider, preventing them from gaining access to the eggs or young nestlings. There is an additional predator guard in place, as the entrance hole is two thicknesses of the faceplate board on the nest box. This prevents a raccoon from reaching his paw inside to grab the eggs or young nestlings.

Vegetation for Backyard Birds
Trees Used Primarily for Food
Abies sp. (fir)
  western scrub and Steller's jay, brown creeper, chickadee, cedar waxwing, flycatcher, finch, junco, kinglet, mourning dove, nuthatch, robin

Acer sp. (maple)
  American goldfinch, cedar waxwing, finch, grosbeak, pine siskin, robin, sparrow, vireo, warbler

Alnus italica (Italian alder)
  American goldfinch, chickadee, finch, mourning dove

Betula nigra (river birch)
American goldfinch, chickadee, finch, mourning dove

Carpinus betulus 'Fastiagata' (European hornbeam)
American goldfinch, finch, grosbeak

Celtis sinensis (hackberry)
cedar waxwing, mockingbird, oriole, robin, thrush, titmouse, thrasher, towhee

Celtus australis (nettle)
cedar waxwing, mockingbird, oriole, robin, thrush, titmouse, thrasher, towhee

Crataegus sp. (hawthorn)
blue, western scrub, and Steller's jays; cedar waxwing, flicker, oriole, pine siskin, robin, thrush, towhee

Ficus sp. (fig)
flicker, grosbeak, oriole, warbler, robin

Fraxinus sp. (ash)
western scrub and Steller's jay, chickadee, cedar waxwing, finch, grosbeak, pine siskin, robin

Juglans sp. (walnut)
western scrub and Steller's jay, flicker, oriole, sparrow, warbler, woodpecker

Liquidambar styraciflua (sweetgum)
American goldfinch, chickadee, finch, mourning dove, pine siskin, sparrow, towhee, woodpecker

Magnolia sp. (magnolia)
robin, thrush, vireo

Malus sp. (crabapple)
American goldfinch, western scrub jay, cedar waxwing, finch, flicker, oriole, robin, towhee, warbler, woodpecker

Quercus sp. (oak)
western scrub and Steller's jay, flicker, oriole, mourning dove, towhee, woodpecker

Picea sp. (spruce)
American goldfinch, chickadee,
cedar waxwing, finch, mourning
dove, pine siskin, sparrow,
woodpecker

Prunus sp. (cherry, plum)
American goldfinch, western
scrub jay, cedar waxwing, finch,
flicker, grosbeak, oriole, robin,
sparrow, thrush, towhee, vireo,
woodpecker

Prunus caroliniana (Carolina cherry)
American goldfinch, western
scrub jay, cedar waxwing, finch,
flicker, grosbeak, oriole, robin,
sparrow, thrush, towhee, vireo,
woodpecker

Prunus ilicifolia (holly leaf cherry)
American goldfinch, western
scrub jay, cedar waxwing, finch,
flicker, grosbeak, oriole, robin,
sparrow, thrush, towhee, vireo,
woodpecker

Prunus lusitanica (Portuguese laurel)
American goldfinch, western

scrub jay, cedar waxwing, finch,
flicker, grosbeak, oriole, robin,
sparrow, thrush, towhee, vireo,
woodpecker

Rhus lancea (African sumac)
California quail

Schinus mollis (California pepper)
cedar waxwing, flicker, robin,
thrush

Umbellaria californica (California bay)
Steller's jay, Townsend's solitaire

Shrubs Used Primarily for Food
Arbutus unedo (strawberry tree)
American robin, western scrub
jay, cedar waxwing

Arctostaphylos sp. (manzanita)
western scrub jay, fox sparrow,
American robin

Arctostaphylos uva-ursi (bearberry)
cedar waxwing, warbler,
American robin, sparrow, thrush

Elaeagnus sp. (Russian olive)
cedar waxwing, finch, flicker,

grosbeak, oriole, robin, sparrow, thrush, towhee, vireo, warbler, woodpecker

Heteromeles arbutifolia (toyon)
California quail

Ilex sp. (holly)
western scrub jay, chickadee, cedar waxwing, finch, flicker, mourning dove, nuthatch, robin, thrush, towhee, vireo, warbler, woodpecker

Ligustrum (privet)
cedar waxwing, finch, sparrow, towhee, wren

Mahonia sp. (Oregon grape)
cedar waxwing, mockingbird, robin, towhee, sparrow

Myrica californica (Pacific wax myrtle)
chickadee, flicker, towhee, warbler

Pyracantha sp. (firethorn)
western scrub jay, cedar waxwing, flicker, nuthatch,

robin, sparrow, thrush, towhee, vireo, woodpecker

Rhamnus californica (coffee berry)
western scrub jay, cedar waxwing, oriole, robin, thrush, warbler

Rhus ovata (sugar bush)
California quail

Ribes sp. (gooseberry)
western scrub jay, finch, flicker, robin, thrush, towhee

Ribes californica; Rosa californica (California gooseberry; California wild rose)
grosbeak, junco, sparrow, Townsend's solitaire, pheasant, California quail

Rubus sp. (blackberry, bramble)
western scrub jay, cedar waxwing, finch, grosbeak, mourning dove, robin, sparrow, thrush, towhee, vireo, warbler

Sambucus sp. (elderberry)
western scrub jay, Steller's jay,

cedar waxwing, finch, flicker,
grosbeak, mourning dove,
nuthatch, California quail, robin,
sparrow, thrush, towhee, vireo,
warbler, woodpecker

Symphoricarpos sp. (snowberry)
cedar waxwing, grosbeak, robin,
thrush, towhee

Vaccinium sp. (huckleberry)
chickadee, robin, flicker, grouse,
Swainson's thrush, waxwings,
California quail

Viburnum sp. (honeysuckle)
cedar waxwing, grosbeak, robin,
sparrow, thrush, towhee, starlings

Vitis sp. (grape)
western scrub jay, cedar
waxwing, finch, mourning dove,
robin, sparrow, thrush

Grasses to Enhance Wild Bird Habitat

Ornamental grasses, especially
native types, attract many birds.

They are used for nesting materials, nesting sites, and seeds for
food. There are many beautiful
grasses to select from. Some of the
birds that are attracted to grasses
include meadowlarks, quail, sparrows, and finches. Here are just a
few of the grasses that seem to be
especially favored:

Andropogon sp. (bluestem)
Arrhenatherum elatius var. *bulbosum*
　(tall oatgrass)
Bouteloua gracilis (blue grama)
Briza sp. (quaking grass)
Cortedaria selloana (pampas grass)
Deschampsia sp. (tufted hair grass)
Elymus sp. (wild rye)
Festuca sp. (fescue)
Miscanthus sp. (maidenhair grass)
Muhlenbergia rigens (deergrass)
Panicum sp. (witchgrass)
Stipa sp. (needlegrass)

Annuals and Perennials Used for Food

Amaranthus sp. (amaranth)
Aquilegia sp. (columbine)
Aster
Calendula officinales (pot marigold)

Campanula sp. (bellflower)
Celosia sp. (cockscomb)
Centaurea cyanus (garden corn-
flower)
Chrysanthemum
Cirsium sp. (thistle)
Coreopsis sp. (tickseed)
Cosmos
Echinacea
Helianthus sp. (sunflower)
Limonium sp. (statice)
Tagetes (marigold)
Myosotis (forget-me-not)
Nigella sp. (love-in-a-mist)
Papaver sp. (poppy)
Phlox sp.
Portulaca sp. (moss rose)
Rudbeckia sp. (black-eyed susan)
Scabiosa sp. (pincushion)
Sedum spectabile (ice plant)
Solidago sp. (goldenrod)
Verbena sp.
Zinnia sp.

Nectar-producing Plants to Attract Hummingbirds

Trees
Aesculus sp. (horse chestnut)

Alibizia julibrissin (silktree)
x Chitalpa tashkentensis (chitalpa)
Citrus
Crataegus sp. (hawthorn)
Melaleuca sp.

Shrubs
Abelia
Arctostaphylos sp. (manzanita)
Buddleia sp. (butterfly bush)
Chaenomeles sp. (flowering quince)
Correa sp. (Australian fuschia)
Diplacus sp. (monkey flower)
Feijoa sallowiana (pineapple guava)
Galvezia speciosa (Bush Island
snapdragon)
Grevellia sp.
Heteromeles arbutifolia (toyon)
Hibiscus syriacus (rose-of-sharon)
Lavandula sp. (lavender)
Jasminum sp. (jasmine)
Kolwitzia sp. (beauty bush)
Lantana
Ribes sp. (gooseberry)
Rosmarinus sp. (rosemary)
Trichostema (bluecurls)
Vitex agnus-castus (chaste tree)
Weigelia
Yucca sp.

Perennials/Annuals

Aguilegia sp. (columbine)
Agave sp.
Alce sp.
Alstroemeria (Peruvian lily)
Ajuga (bugleweed)
Althea sp. (hollyhock)
Antirrhinum (snapdragon)
Asclepias tuberosa (butterfly weed)
Castilleja sp. (Indian paintbrush)
Dahlia
Delphinium
Dianthus
Digitalis purpurea (foxglove)
Echium fastuosum (pride of madeira)
Fuschia
Gladiolus
Hemerocallis (daylily)
Heuchera
Impatiens balsamina (balsam)
Ipomopsis
Iris
Kniphofia (red hot poker)
Lilium
Lobelia cardinalis (cardinalflower)
Lupinus (lupine)

Marabilis
Monarda didyma (scarlet beebalm)
Nicotiana
Oenothera
Pelargonium
Penstemon (beard tongue)
Petunia
Phaseolus coccineus (scarlet runner bean)
Phygelius (cape fuschia)
Salvia sp. (sage)
Saponaria (soapwort)
Tropaeolum sp. (nasturtium)
Verbena
Zauschneria sp. (California fuschia)
Zinnia

Vines

Campsis radicans (trumpet vine)
Cestrum elegans (red cestrum)
Distictis buccinatoria (blood red trumpet vine)
Ipomoea
Lonicera (honeysuckle)
Tecomaria capensis (cape honey-suckle)

Creating a Safe Experience for Birds Visiting Your Feeder
—David J. Horn, Director of Research, Wild Bird Centers of America

In 1999, thousands of American crows died with the arrival of West Nile Virus in New York City. The virus quickly spread, reaching the West Coast in 2003. As the virus spread from coast to coast, tens of thousands of birds died including hawks, jays, and chickadees. Fortunately for people who feed birds, West Nile Virus is not known to be transmitted from bird to feeder to bird contact; rather, the predominant mode of transmission is from mosquito to bird.

There are, however, several diseases that birds can acquire at feeding stations if they are not properly cared for, and it is important for people who feed birds to create a backyard environment that is safe for our feathered friends. Follow the described steps recommended by the National Wildlife Health Center (www.nwhc.usgs.gov) to reduce the risk of disease to birds using your feeders.

First, provide birds with a large amount of space for feeding. Birds crowded onto a single feeder increase the likelihood of contact between sick and healthy birds, and may increase a bird's stress level while feeding, making them more susceptible to disease. One solution would be to purchase feeders that minimize contact between birds. Overcrowding at feeders may also be alleviated by providing birds with other places to feed.

A second step is to keep the birds' feeding area free of a buildup of seed hulls and bird droppings by cleaning the area below the feeder. One way to minimize the cleaning needed would be to use no-waste seeds or seed mixes that contain hulled seeds, and to only offer the preferred seeds for the bird species in your area.

Third, purchase feeders that do not have sharp points or edges. Such feeders may cause bleeding or scratches on birds that can result in the transmission of disease.

Regularly cleaning your feeders is the fourth step you can take. Feeders should be washed approximately once a month with a solution of 10 percent bleach (one part bleach to nine parts water) by completely immersing feeders for at least three minutes and then allowing them to dry. Purchasing feeders that are made of materials that are easier to clean, such as metal and plastic, may also make cleaning the feeder easier.

Finally, store food appropriately and ensure that fresh seed is in your feeder. Use a rodent-proof container to store food, and avoid having wet, moldy, musty-smelling seed in your feeder. Providing feeders that protect the seed from the elements and placing seeds that birds in your area prefer should reduce the chance of seed getting wet or moldy.

In addition to the above steps, people who provide water to birds should scrub their bird bath and change the water in their bath several times per week to prevent mosquito reproduction and the possible spread of West Nile Virus.

Bird feeding is a wonderful pastime and it provides those who feed birds with a greater connection to the natural world we live in. Providing a safe and clean feeding environment will allow you to enjoy our feathered friends while lowering the risk to birds of disease at feeders.

To learn more about additional ways to improve the bird feeding experience, download a copy of the 6 steps to turn your yard into a sanctuary for birds brochure on the Wild Bird Centers of America Web site (http://www.wildbirdcenter.com/cms/www_files/6ways.pdf).

Fun Bird Projects

A fun project for the individual or family is to keep a backyard bird list. Each time a new bird species arrives in my backyard bird sanctuary, I record it on my "backyard bird list." Over the last twenty-one years that I have lived in our present home I have recorded new birds visiting the backyard bird sanctuary. The list stands today at eighty-seven different bird species.

Over that same time period, I have continued to make improvements to the habitat. Trees that I planted twenty-one years ago have become substantial cover assets for the birds today. Nearly all of my plantings produce a crop of some sort. It might be crabapples, berries, grapes, acorns, or blossoms that produce. They also provide a harbor for insects, their larvae, and cocoons. The birds will enjoy foraging among the cover to discover what might be there for them to eat.

Nesting, loafing, and roosting cover is available for them too. There are several water features from the traditional pedestal bath to a mister, water dripper, and recycling pump that keep the water moving. The water dripper performs two functions: it moves water and replaces water lost through evaporation or splashing of bathing birds. Included in the water features are several rocks that I have placed to create structure and differing depth levels. Some birds like the robins will jump right into the deep end of the bath. Others like the American goldfinch like the shallow end of the bath. Chickadees like to pick up drops of water coming from the dripper. The pedestal bath is allowed to overflow into a ground-level bath below it, so that the doves, quail, and other ground-feeding birds can access the water. Present water and food at the level that mimics the bird's natural behavior. Doing so will reward you with birds flocking to your backyard bird sanctuary.

Additionally, I keep a list of when the different bird species arrive in my backyard bird sanctuary. This helps me to be prepared for those migratory species that I may only see for a short period of time. Lazuli buntings arrive in my backyard by April 1. I make sure that the platform feeder has ample white proso millet for them. April 15 brings a smile to my face while many others may be fretting and grimacing over their tax return. The hummingbirds are back. Nectar feeders are cleaned and hung with fresh nectar. May 1 will bring orioles. The mealworms, grape jelly, and orange halves are out and waiting for them. The red hot poker flowers are beginning to bloom. I have hung a ball of wool and cotton for nesting material that the oriole will pick at when making its basket-shaped nest in our cottonwood. The Bullock's oriole will find everything ready and the table set for his arrival. June is nesting and fledging time. Robins will be bringing their young onto the lawn where they will hunt worms. Young quail are following their mom through the scrub oak. They can leave the nest and begin following mom and foraging a few hours after hatching. July is a time for young to grow and stretch their wings. Some of the birds begin to molt. Goldfinches are late nesters and are bringing newly fledged young to the Nyjer feeders filled with those tiny black seeds bursting with oil. August and September begin to show early migration in some of the birds. Orioles will soon depart, as well as the hummingbirds. The Neotropical birds put on an extra layer of fat at my feeders in preparation for the migration that will take them far to the south, some as far as Central and South America. October arrives and I clean out the nest boxes so that they will be ready for use as winter roosting areas. The entrance hole is moved from the top of the box to the bottom. The air vents are closed and the old nest removed. Suet is placed in the feeders for the flickers and ruby-crowned kinglets that will winter in my yard. House finches eagerly take the black oil sunflower seeds I place in my MoBi Mesh Feeder.

The spotted towhee arrives with winter's first snowstorm in November. His migration is one of elevation. Deepening snow higher up on the mountain forces this ground feeder down into sheltered valleys. My backyard is an ideal wintering area for him. My brush pile, low-growing shrubs, and Oregon grapevine tangle are ready to provide him the cover he desires, as well as areas to scratch about for seeds. Seed has been scattered under the brush pile for him to find. White-crowned sparrows arrive with the towhees. Dark-eyed juncos arrive soon after the towhees. Downy woodpeckers and black-capped chickadees form mixed foraging flocks with these sparrows. Together they will winter in the brush piles, hedges, shrubs, and thickets in the backyard. December shows that winter is here in earnest. Snow is deepening in the yard. I have shoveled a path around to the feeders from my garden shed where I store my seed in galvanized cans. Bright orange pyracantha berries are attracting cedar waxwings to the backyard sanctuary now. The grandchildren press their noses against the cold of the glass window as they watch the birds at the feeders. Quail and pheasant tracks are in my shoveled pathway. They use it so they can avoid slogging through the deeper snow. January is announced by the hooting of a great horned owl. A few nights later I hear the whinny of a screech owl. The owl breeding season will soon be here. My nest box for the screech owl has two inches of fresh wood shavings in it. There are two boxes set up in my scrub oak grove. The male will use one and keep watch over the female who will use the other. I have them placed so that he can see the entrance hole of his mate. Her box faces east so that she will have morning sun. He will receive the afternoon sun with his westerly facing roosting box. February is cold, yet there is a hint of warmer times not far off. Melting icicles hint of the spring thaw just around the corner. Black oil sunflower and Nyjer are favorites for the seed eaters. Suet provides energy for the insect-eating ruby-crowned kinglet that has remained in the backyard throughout the winter. Every once in a while I catch a glimpse of his neon red crown that he flashes. It is another hint that spring is not far away. Pheasant and quail march through the snow on my pathway to the ground feeders. The heated bird bath has lots of action throughout the day from birds who stop for a drink, as well as the robins and waxwings who bathe contentedly. March dawns and I hear the house finch singing as the morning sun warms the birds. His song signals that winter is loosening its grip and spring will soon prevail. Spring will bring the breeding season and new birds will soon arrive on their migration. Winter residents prepare to leave and the cycle begins anew.

Who needs a calendar to tell them what time of year it is? The natural rhythms and cycles let me know what time it is and what to expect next. I have reversed the convertible nest box so the chickadees will find it ready for their new nest. House wrens are singing. The flicker has started to drum on our wood-burning stove stack. The machine-gun staccato of his drumming wakes me this morning. My wife asks me, "Who is knocking at the door?" "Spring," I answer. "Spring is here."

Citizen Science Programs

The Cornell Lab of Ornithology and the National Audubon Society have a wonderful array of citizen science programs for the family or the individual bird lover. You can contact the Cornell Lab of Ornithology at www.birds.cornell.edu/. Here is a brief list of some of their programs:

- nest-box monitoring project
- informal science education
- continent-wide research
- proactive conservation

- information related to cavity-nesting birds
- online nest-box cam
- Project Classroom feeder watch

Contact the National Audubon Society at www.audubon.org. They have local regional chapters that you can consider joining. These chapters engage in a variety of local conservation projects that benefit birds and other wildlife. Audubon conducted the 107th Christmas Bird Count in 2007. These projects help scientists in learning about long-range trends in bird populations: whether they are shrinking, expanding, or remaining the same.

Birds are a key indicator species. They can act as an early-warning system when something is wrong in our environment. Other birding and conservation groups that can provide additional information include:

- The Nature Conservancy (www.nature.org) is a wonderful national organization that promotes conservation and saving habitat. It has nature trails and has protected key species around the country with its important work.
- The American Birding Association (www.americanbirding.org) is an organization for those who want to become more serious in their study of birds.
- The American Bird Conservancy (www.abcbirds.org) maintains a Bird Conservation Alliance that helps group in furthering our knowledge and conservation work with birds.

Allen's
Hummingbird
page 19

Anna's
Hummingbird
page 23

Rufous
Hummingbird
page 21

Lesser
Goldfinch
page 27

Bushtit
page 25

American
Goldfinch
page 29

Pine Siskin
page 31

Oak
Titmouse
page 33

House
Finch
page 35

Dark-eyed
Junco
page 37

House
Sparrow
page 39

Downy
Woodpecker
page 41

Golden-
crowned
Sparrow
page 43

Black-
headed
Grosbeak
page 45

93

European Starling
page 49

Bullock's
Oriole
page 47

California
Towhee
page 51

American
Robin
page 53

Northern
Mockingbird
page 55

Western
Scrub Jay
page 57

Mourning
Dove
page 59

Northern
Flicker
(Red-shafted)
page 61

Sharp-shinned Hawk
page 63

American
Crow
page 65

Cooper's
Hawk
page 67

Backyard Birds across the country!

Soon to include all 50 states.
Available in stores nationwide or directly from

Gibbs Smith, Publisher
1.800.835.4993/www.gibbs-smith.com